canoe

footprints

gun

hut

kiss

raft

Note about the story

Mark Twain (Samuel Langhorne Clemens) lived from 1835 until 1910. He was from Missouri in the middle of the United States.

The Adventures of Huckleberry Finn (1884) is the story of a boy on the long Mississippi River in the 1840s. Huckleberry Finn lives in St. Petersburg—a village next to the river. Mark Twain's first book about Huckleberry Finn was *The Adventures of Tom Sawyer* (1876), also in the Penguin Readers series at Level 2.

Until 1865, there were **slaves*** in some parts of the United States. White people took black people from Africa, and they made them slaves. In those days, nearly all the black people in America were slaves. There were not many **free** black people.

Before-reading questions

1 Look at the cover of the book. What do you think will happen in this story?

2 What do you know about Mark Twain's books and the movies about his stories?

3 Read the names of the chapters on page 3. Which chapters are the most interesting to you? Why?

4 Look at the people in the story on page 4. Choose one of the people and describe him or her. What is he or she like?

*Definitions of words in **bold** can be found in the glossary on page 63.

Contents

WITHDRAWN FROM STOCK

People in the story

Huckleberry Finn

Tom Sawyer

Jim

The Duke

The King

Aunt Sally

CHAPTER ONE

Meet Huck Finn

Do you know a book called *The Adventures of Tom Sawyer?* It is about me, Huckleberry Finn, my friend Tom Sawyer, and the village of St. Petersburg. We found $6,000.

Judge Thatcher took the money to the bank, and the bank gave us a dollar every day. That is more money than one boy can use.

Tom Sawyer's mother and father were **dead**, and my mother was dead, too. My father was never there. I had no home, and I was often hungry. But I was **free** and happy. Nobody told me to wash or go to school or wear shoes. I could fight and go to sleep late. I could do everything my **way**.

But after our **adventures**, I lived with Widow Douglas. She was a kind, old woman, but living her way was difficult for me. After a year, it was a little easier.

Widow Douglas and I lived with her sister, Miss Watson. There was also a black man called Jim. He was Miss Watson's **slave**, and he worked for the family.

Sometimes, I went to school, and now I could read and write a little.

One morning, I left the house, and I saw footprints in the snow near the front door. I knew these footprints—they were my father's.

I ran to Judge Thatcher's house.

"Are you here for your money?" he asked.

"No," I said. "I don't want any of it. I want to give it to you—all six thousand dollars."

He did not understand. "What's the matter, boy?"

"Please. You take it all. And don't ask me any questions."

"Oh, I think I understand," he said.

Judge Thatcher wrote something on paper, and then he said, "I'll give you one dollar for all your money."

I wrote my name on the paper.

That night, I went up to my bedroom. There, on my bed, sat my father.

Dad was an old man now. His hair was long and dirty, and his face was very white.

"They're very nice clothes," he said. "You're a big man now, aren't you?"

"Maybe I am; maybe I'm not," I said.

"Shut up! I'll tell you now. You're *nothing*!"

He was quiet again. Then he said, "Can you read now? Show me!"

I opened a book and read something about George

Washington. Dad took the book, and he hit me on the head with it.

"You stop going to that school, boy, do you understand? Your mother couldn't read. I can't read. You're not better than any of us. And look at you. You've got this bed, and your father sleeps with animals on the ground. And you're rich!"

"It's not true," I said.

"I heard about it everywhere. I came here because of that money. Give it to me tomorrow."

"I don't have any money. Ask Judge Thatcher," I said.

"I will. And he'll give it to me, or . . . How much money have you got now?" he asked.

"I've only got a dollar, and I want that to—"

"Give it to me."

He took the money, and he went out of the window.

CHAPTER TWO
Escape!

Judge Thatcher did not give Dad any money. I went to school nearly every day now, because Dad told me not to go. He hit me, and I went to school more.

Dad often came to Widow Douglas's house. **Finally**, she said to him, "You have to leave. Go or I'll make problems for you. I'll get Judge Thatcher."

Well, Dad did not like that. "You're not Huck's parent," he said. "*I'm* Huck's parent. I'll show you."

———

One day in the spring, Dad waited for me after school, and he caught me. He took me across the river to a hut in the trees. I could not **escape** because he was always with me. At night, he closed the door, and he put the key under his head in bed. He also had a gun.

I liked it in the hut for the first two months. There was no school, and there were no books. We ate fish from the river, and we **shot** small animals with the gun.

I did not want to go back to St. Petersburg now. How did I live at the widow's? How did I always wash every morning and eat from a plate? Why did I always listen to Miss Watson?

But then Dad started to hit me more and more. And he often went away. He left me in the hut, and he took the key with him.

Sometimes, I was in the hut for three days with no food. I tried to escape, but I could not.

————

One day, Dad was away, and I found a knife in the hut. I started to **dig** under the wall. But then I heard Dad, and I **hid** my work.

That night, Dad shouted, and he tried to fight me. Finally, he went to sleep. I took his gun because I was frightened of him.

In the morning, he was angry because I had the gun.

"Somebody tried to come into the hut," I said.

"Well, you must wake me up," he said. "I'll shoot the next man with my gun. Now, go and look for fish in the river."

On the river, I found a beautiful canoe. I hid it and went to get the fish.

That night, Dad was away, and I finished digging under the wall. I carried some food to the canoe.

I went back to the hut and hit the hut door with the gun again and again. Finally, it opened.

I found a pig near the hut, and I shot it. In the hut, I cut the pig with the knife. The animal's red **blood** ran all over the floor. I pulled some hair from my head and put it with the blood. Then I hid the dead pig in the river.

I went to sleep in the canoe, and I woke up late in the night. Everything was very quiet; then I heard something.

Across the river, I saw a small boat with a man in it. It was Dad! I quietly escaped in the canoe.

I knew a good place to stay. It was two or three **miles** down the river from St. Petersburg. I could hide there, and I could hide the canoe, too.

From my place in the trees, I could see the river. In the afternoon, a boat went past. Everyone was on it: Dad, Judge Thatcher, Tom Sawyer, and his **Aunt** Polly, and his brother Sid, and more people.

"They're looking for my dead body in the river," I thought.

I hid, and I waited. Finally, the boat went back to St. Petersburg.

Now, I was free.

CHAPTER THREE
Down the river

On the third day, I saw a man by a fire—someone was here! It was Miss Watson's slave, Jim.

"Hello, Jim!" I said.

He was very frightened to see me. "But you're dead," he said. "Please don't do anything bad to me."

"It's OK, Jim. I'm not dead," I said.

"But Huck, what happened in the hut?"

I told him the story.

"That was a very good plan," Jim said. "Tom Sawyer couldn't make a better plan than that."

Jim and I ate some fish for breakfast.

"Why are you here, Jim?" I asked him.

"Well, you won't tell anyone, will you, Huck?"

"Of course not, Jim."

"I . . . I escaped," he said.

"Jim!" I shouted.

"Remember—you won't tell!" said Jim.

"Yes, I did say that. You did a bad thing, but I won't tell. I *can't* tell because I'll never go back to St. Petersburg. Why did you escape?"

THE ADVENTURES OF HUCKLEBERRY FINN

"Well, one day, a man came from New Orleans," said Jim. "He wanted slaves. Miss Watson told the Widow, 'I can get eight hundred dollars for Jim.' I heard her, and then I ran."

———

For ten days it rained, and the river was very high. The rain pushed many things into the river. One night, Jim and I went out in the canoe, and we found a small house in the river. We went into the house through a window. There was a dead man on the floor.

"Don't look at him," Jim said to me. "Someone shot him."

I didn't want to look at the body, but we took some clothes and food from the house. We also found a raft on the river.

We lived very well on the river. But I wanted news from St. Petersburg, and I made a plan to go there. We had some girls' clothes from the house in the river.

One night, I took them, and I went to the village in the canoe.

I wore the girls' clothes. Through a window, I saw a woman. I did not know her face—she was new in St. Petersburg. "Come in," said the woman. "What's your name?"

"Sarah Williams," I answered.

"Where do you live?" she asked.

"In Hookerville. I walked for two hours, and I'm very tired."

We talked, and she told me about Huck Finn, and Tom Sawyer, and the money.

"And then someone killed Huck," she said.

"Who killed him?" I asked.

"Well, maybe it was his father," she answered.

"No!" I said.

"Or maybe it was a slave called Jim," she said.

"Why, he—"

"That slave escaped the same night," she said. "People are looking for them. They can get money for finding them—three hundred dollars for Jim and two hundred dollars for the father. What's your name, again?"

"M . . . Mary Williams," I said.

"You said Sarah," she said.

"Oh, yes, I did. "Sarah Mary Williams. Some people say Sarah, some people say Mary."

"You're not a girl. You're a boy," she said.

I went back to the raft quickly. "Jim! Quick, Jim!" I shouted. "Wake up! They're looking for us!"

Jim and I traveled down the great Mississippi River on our raft for many days. We traveled at night, and Jim hid in the day. Every morning, we found a good place to hide.

CHAPTER FOUR
A duke and a king

One morning, two men ran onto our raft. One man was young, and the other was old. They wanted to escape from some men and their dogs.

They were not good men. They traveled from town to town, and they **tricked** people. Then they took their money.

"It's very sad for me to be here on this raft," the young man told us. "I'm a **duke**."

"Wow!" said Jim.

"Yes," the young man said. "My English grandfather was the Duke of Bridgewater. His oldest son came to America. He had a son here—me—and then he died. The Duke in England also died. The dead Duke's second son—my **uncle**—tricked everyone. He told everyone, 'I'm the next Duke because my dead older brother had no children.' But I'm the true Duke," said the young man, and he started to cry. "But I'm a poor man in old, dirty clothes."

Jim and I were sorry for him, but what could we do?

"You can say 'My Lord' or 'Bridgewater' to me," the Duke said. "And you can do everything for me."

Jim and I started to do everything for the Duke, but the old man did not like that. He was very quiet all morning. That afternoon, he spoke.

"Look, Bridgewater," he said. "I'm very sorry for you. But you're not the only important person here. I'm a **king**!"

"What?" asked the Duke.

"Yes, I'm the King of France," said the old man. "I'm Louis the Seventeenth—the son of Louis the Sixteenth and Marie Antoinette. Nobody knows the true story. I didn't die. I escaped from France."

Well, now Jim and I did everything for the Duke and for the King because we were frightened of them. Of course, they were not dukes or kings, I knew that. They were bad men. But we were together on a small raft now, and it is easier to live with happy men. I learned that from Dad.

The Duke, the King, Jim, and I traveled together down the river. One day, our raft came to a town called Pokeville.

It was Sunday, and there was a **preacher** there. He sang, and the people all sang with him.

Then the preacher shouted, and he put his arms up. Everyone shouted and put their arms up, too.

The King shouted with all the people, and then he went and stood with the preacher. The preacher asked him to speak.

"I was a **pirate**," the King said, "for thirty years in the Indian Ocean. Yesterday, someone took all my money. Now I have nothing, but I'm happy. I'm a new man, and I have a new plan. I'm going to go back to the ocean, and I'm going to talk to all the pirates. I'll change them into good men. It's a long way to go, and I don't have any money. But help me, and I'll do it. And I'll say the same thing to every pirate. I'll say, 'Don't thank me. Thank the good people in Pokeville. Thank the preacher there. He's the truest friend of pirates!'"

The King started to cry, and everyone cried, too. People put money into a hat for him.

The King cried more, and he thanked everyone. The prettiest girls kissed him.

Everyone wanted the King to stay in their houses, but he said, "I'm going back to the Indian Ocean today."

On the raft, the King counted his money. He had
$87. He bought us all some new clothes.

CHAPTER FIVE
Tricking a family

We looked very good in our new, clean clothes. Near the next town, we met a young man.

"I'm waiting for a boat to New Orleans, and then I'm going to Brazil," he told us. "I know you," the man said to the King. "You're Harvey Wilks!"

"No, I'm not Harvey Wilks," answered the King.

"Oh," said the man. "That's good because there's bad news for Harvey. His brother, Peter, is dead."

The young man told us all about the Wilks family. "There were four brothers in England," he said. "The oldest two—George and Peter—came to America. Harvey and William were only young children, and they stayed in England with their parents. In America, George married and had three daughters. He and his wife died, and then their daughters lived with their Uncle Peter. Peter was a good father to them."

"What about the English brothers?" asked the King.

"Harvey is a preacher," answered the man. "Poor William can't hear anything, and he can't speak."

"Did they see their American brothers again?" asked the King.

"No, never," said the man. "Peter was ill for months. He wrote to his brothers because he wanted to see them. Maybe they are traveling here now, but they are too late."

The King asked the man many more questions about the Wilks family. Then the New Orleans boat came, and the man left. But the King remembered everything, because he had a new plan.

We all traveled to the Wilks's village. The King, the Duke, and I looked for the Wilks family. Jim hid with the raft.

"Where does Peter Wilks live?" the King asked someone. "I'm his brother, Harvey Wilks." Then he pointed at the Duke. "And this is William."

"I'm sorry. We can show you Peter Wilks's house, but he's not there. He died in the night," the man said, sadly.

"Our poor brother!" said the King, and he started to cry.

The King told the Duke about Peter with his hands, and the Duke began to cry, too. I did not enjoy watching it. The King and the Duke were very bad men. I was sorry for all the people in the village.

The news traveled quickly through the village. Lots of people came to the Wilks's house because they wanted to see us. Peter's three **nieces** were inside the house. Of course, the King now knew their names and everything about them. Mary Jane was nineteen. Susan was fifteen. Joanna was fourteen.

"Hello, we're Harvey and William," said the King.

"Uncle Harvey! Uncle William!" said Mary Jane. "We're very happy to meet you. Our uncle told us all about you."

"And he wrote to us about you," said the King, and he cried again. "I'm sorry. We were too late to see our brother. But we're here now. Everything will be OK, girls. Can I see my poor brother?"

Mary Jane took the two men into the room with Peter Wilks's body. They saw him, and they cried and they cried. I never saw anyone cry as loudly as that. I felt terrible.

Peter left a letter for Harvey, and the King read it to everyone. He read, "I, Peter Wilks, give my house and three thousand dollars to my nieces. To my brothers, Harvey and William, I give three thousand dollars and my farm, and all my other things."

The King and the Duke found Peter's money in the house. The King gave all $6,000 to Peter's nieces in front of everybody.

"We cannot take this," the King said. "You three must have it all. All the money is yours."

The three sisters were very happy, and they kissed the King and the Duke.

Then Peter Wilks's doctor spoke. "You're not Harvey Wilks! You're not English!" he said angrily to the King.

"You're wrong, doctor," said Mary Jane sweetly, "He *is* Harvey. He knows everybody's names, and he brought his brother, William, with him. And look, he's giving us all the money."

"Mary Jane," said the doctor, loudly. "Listen to me. Send these men away! They're tricking you."

"Here's my answer," Mary Jane said. "Uncle Harvey, please take all our money. Put it in the bank for us."

Now the King and the Duke had all Peter's money. Then they got more money from Peter's farm and other things.

But I was very unhappy. Peter's nieces were very kind to me. I did not want the King and the Duke to trick them. I wanted to help the girls.

But then the true Harvey and William Wilks came to the town. I quickly ran away. Jim and I started to leave on the raft, but then the Duke and the King got onto the raft with us, too.

We traveled down the river again. Now we were hundreds of miles from St. Petersburg. After some days, we stopped at a new place. I went into the nearest town. I came back to the raft, but the Duke, the King, and Jim were not there. Where was Jim? I had to find him!

"Did you see a slave near here?" I asked a boy.

"Yes," he said. "Some men took him to Silas Phelps's farm near here. Mr. Phelps gave them forty dollars for the slave."

I had to go to this farm and find Jim.

CHAPTER SIX
A great plan

Phelps's farm was very quiet in the hot sun. I did not have time to make a plan because some dogs ran towards me. A woman came out of the kitchen, and she shouted at the dogs. Then another woman came out of the house. Some children came with her, and they hid behind her skirt.

"It's *you*! Isn't it?" the woman smiled at me. She pulled me into her arms and kissed me.

"Yes," I said. I did not know her. She held me strongly, and she cried.

"I'm very happy to see you, Tom!" she said. "Finally, you're here! It's me — I'm your Aunt Sally. You look much bigger and you're very different from your mother. Lizzie, go and get Tom a hot breakfast."

In the house, the woman sat at the table with me. "We waited a long time for your visit," she said. "Why are you two days late? Was there a problem with the boat?"

"Yes," I answered. Who *were* these people and what were they talking about? I did not know.

"Now, tell me about my sister, Polly, and all the family. How are they? What are they doing? Tell me everything."

What could I say? What a problem! This game had to finish. I had to tell the true story.

I started to speak, but then the woman pushed me behind a chair.

"Silas is coming!" she said. "Let's trick him. Hide and be quiet. Children, don't say a word."

An old man came into the house. "Did Tom come?" she asked him.

"No," the man answered.

"Oh dear!" she said. "Where can he be?"

"I don't know," said the man. "I'm frightened for him."

The woman talked and talked. Then she said, brightly, "Why, Silas! Look at the road! Is someone coming?"

He went to the window, and she pulled me from behind the chair. The old man saw me.

"Why, who's that?" he said.

"Who do you think?" the woman asked.

"Why, I don't know! Who *is* it?" he asked.

"It's Tom Sawyer!"

"*What?*" I thought. It was not possible! Sally was Tom Sawyer's aunt! The man took my hand, and the woman laughed and cried. Then they asked me questions about Sally's sister, Aunt Polly, and Tom's brother, Sid, and everyone in the family.

I told them all about the Sawyer family, but I had a problem. Where was the true Tom Sawyer? I had to go into town and find him quickly. He must not come to the Phelps's house.

I met Tom Sawyer on the road into the town. He was frightened to see me.

"But you're dead," he said.

"I'm not dead," I told him. "You can feel me."

He felt my body, and he was happier. I told him about the problem of the two Tom Sawyers.

He thought about it. "That's OK," he said. "I have a plan. I won't be Tom, I'll be my brother, Sid. Go back to the house now, and I'll come in a minute."

"OK, but there's one more thing," I told him. "There's a slave here. I want to help him. His name is Jim—Old Miss Watson's Jim."

"What!" Tom said, "Why, Jim is—"

"It's a bad thing to help him, I know, but I'm going to do it. Please don't tell anyone."

Tom's eyes were bright. "I'll help you!" he said.

I went back to the house and after five minutes Tom came to the door.

"Mr. Archibald Nichols?" Tom said to Silas Phelps.

"No, my boy," said the old man, kindly. "Mr. Nichols doesn't live here. Come in and rest. Then we'll take you to him."

Tom came into the house, and he kissed Aunt Sally! She was very angry.

"Why did you do that?!" she shouted.

"I wanted to make you happy," Tom said.

"Why will that make me happy?" Aunt Sally asked.

"I don't understand," replied Tom. "I thought, 'I'll kiss her. She'll like it.'"

Aunt Sally was very angry, and she wanted to hit Tom.

Tom stood up. "I'm sorry. I won't do it again," he said.

"Of course you won't!" answered Aunt Sally.

"No. I won't do it again. You'll have to ask me to kiss you."

"Ask you?" she said. "I'll never ask you to kiss me. Never!"

"But it's me, Aunt Sally, Sid. I'm Sid Sawyer, Tom Sawyer's brother!" Tom said.

"Why, you tricked me, Sid!" Aunt Sally said, quickly.

She tried to kiss him, but he said, "Remember! You have to ask me first!"

She laughed, and she kissed him again and again. Then Silas did the same.

Aunt Sally wanted to be angry about "Sid's" game, but she was too happy.

CHAPTER SEVEN

A big adventure

That night, Tom told me, "Jim's in a hut behind the house. A slave took some food in there for him. He opened the hut door with Uncle Silas's key."

"That's good," I said.

"Now," said Tom. "You think of a plan to take Jim. I'll make a plan, too, and then we can choose the best one."

"My plan is easy," I said. "Tomorrow, I'll get the canoe and the raft ready. Then we'll leave at night. We'll take the key from Uncle Silas's pants. We'll take Jim from the hut, and we'll go away down the river. Will that work?"

"*Work*?" said Tom. "Why, it'll work, but it's too easy. What good is an easy plan? It has to be difficult!"

The hut had a small window. "Look, Tom," I said. "We can open this window for Jim."

"That's too easy, too," Tom said. "We need a better plan."

I did not say anything because Tom always knows best. One of his plans is better than fifteen of mine.

"I know. We can dig Jim out," said Tom.

We had to dig for days, but Tom made it a big adventure. Finally, everything was ready.

"Now," Tom said, "It's time for the letter."

"What letter?" I asked.

"We have to tell people about the plan, Huck! They do it in all the books. That's what makes it an adventure."

Tom wrote the letter, and pushed it under the door.

Some men will take your slave.
They will come tonight at 12 a.m.
Be ready.
FROM A FRIEND

The family was very frightened. Uncle Silas and Aunt Sally put a man by the door, and he watched everything. I did not like it, but Tom was happy.

"It's good news," he said, "We're doing everything the right way."

That night, fifteen men with guns came to the house. Uncle Silas asked them because of the letter. Tom was in the hut with Jim. I had to tell Tom about the men!

I ran to the hut. "Quick, Tom!" I said. "We have to go, now! There are fifteen men in the house with guns."

"Wow!" Tom's eyes were big.

We quickly left the hut. Jim went first, then me, then Tom. But Tom made a little noise.

"Who's that?" shouted one of the men.

We did not answer. We ran, and we heard the guns. *BANG! BANG! BANG!*

"There they are!" someone shouted. "They're going to the river. Go after them! And send the dogs!"

The dogs ran towards us. But they were friendly because they knew us from the village. At the river, we got onto the raft.

"Now, Jim. You're a *free* man," I said. "You won't be a slave again."

"You boys did a good job," Jim said.

But then Tom said, "There's blood on my leg. Someone shot me." Jim and I tried to help him.

"Let's go," said Tom.

But Jim said, "I'm not going. You need a doctor."

I ran to town to find a doctor. He was a kind, old man. He helped Tom, but then he took everyone back to Aunt Sally's house.

After two days in bed, Tom woke up. I was in the room with Aunt Sally.

"Hello! Did you tell Aunt Sally?" Tom asked me.

"What are you talking about?" asked Aunt Sally.

"We tried to help Jim to escape," Tom said. "And we did it beautifully, too. And I—oh it's Tom's AUNT POLLY!"

Aunt Polly was at the door! I hid under the bed because Aunt Polly knew me.

"Tom," asked Aunt Polly. "How are you?"

"That's not Tom," said Aunt Sally to her sister, "that's Sid. Tom is—Tom is—why, where *is* Tom?"

"You mean, 'where's *Huck Finn*?'" said Aunt Polly. "Come out from under the bed, Huck."

Then everyone learned the true story. I also learned about Jim. "Miss Watson is dead," said Aunt Polly. "And she made Jim free. He is a free man now."

Tom and I wanted to go on an adventure again, but I needed money.

"Your dad couldn't take your money from Judge Thatcher because the judge bought it from you," Tom told me. "But he will give it back to you now."

"And your dad won't come back, Huck," said Jim.

"Why?" I asked.

"Do you remember that house in the river with the body in it?" Jim said. "That was your dad. Your money is safe."

Now Aunt Sally wants me to live with her, but I do not want to live with more women. I want to live my way.

During-reading questions

Write the answers to these questions in your notebook.

CHAPTER ONE

1 Who is Jim?
2 What does Huck see in the snow?
3 How much money does Judge Thatcher give Huck?

CHAPTER TWO

1 Why does Huck start going to school more often?
2 Where does Huck's father take Huck?
3 What does Huck find on the river?
4 How does Huck escape from the hut?

CHAPTER THREE

1 Who does Huck meet by a fire?
2 How much money can Miss Watson get for Jim?
3 What does Huck wear to visit St. Petersburg?

CHAPTER FOUR

1 Two men come onto the raft. How do these men get
   their money?
2 The two men are not kings or dukes, but Huck does everything
   for them. Why does he do that, do you think?
3 Where do Huck, the King and the Duke meet the preacher?
4 What does the King buy everyone?

CHAPTER FIVE

1 They meet a young man near the next town. Where is he going?
2 Which Wilks brothers first came to America from England?
3 Why is Huck sorry for all the people in the village?
4 How far is Huck from St. Petersburg?

CHAPTER SIX

1 Where do the children hide?
2 Who is Aunt Sally's sister?
3 Who does Aunt Sally trick?
4 Why does Huck go into town?

CHAPTER SEVEN

1 Where does Huck put the letter?
2 Why does Huck hide under the bed?
3 Who was the dead man in the house in the river?

After-reading questions

1 Huck's father says, "You're a big man now, aren't you?" Why does he say this to Huck?
2 Why does Huck want to give all his money to Judge Thatcher, do you think?
3 Why does Huck kill a pig?
4 Why can Huck and Jim only travel at night?
5 Huck says, "It is easier to live with happy men. I learned that from Dad." What does this tell you about Huck's father?
6 The King talks to the Duke with his hands. Why does he do this?
7 Why do you think Tom kisses Aunt Sally?
8 Why do you think Tom says, "What good is an easy plan? It has to be difficult!"

Exercises

CHAPTER ONE

1 **Are these sentences *true* or *false*? Write the correct sentences in your notebook.**

1 Huckleberry Finn and Tom Sawyer lost $6,000. ....*false*........

2 After his adventures, Huck lives with Widow Douglas.

3 Miss Watson is Jim's slave.

4 Huck Finn wants to give Judge Thatcher all his money.

5 Huck's father reads the book in Huck's bedroom.

6 Huck's father sleeps with animals on the ground.

CHAPTER TWO

2 **Write the past tense of these irregular verbs in your notebook.**

1 Dad waited for me after school, and he ...*caught*... (catch) me.

2 We .... (eat) fish from the river, and we .... (shoot) small animals with the gun.

3 He .... (leave) me in the hut, and he .... (take) the key with him to the village.

4 But then I .... (hear) Dad, and I .... (hide) my work.

5 "Somebody .... (try) to come into the hut," I .... (say).

6 I .... (go) to sleep in the canoe, and I .... (wake up) late in the night.

3 Complete these sentences in your notebook, using the words from the box.

Every morning,	One night,	One day,
For ten days	the same night	On the third day,

1 _On the third day_ I saw a man by a fire.
2 .... a man came from New Orleans. He wanted slaves.
3 .... it rained, and the river was very high.
4 .... I took the canoe to the village.
5 That slave escaped ....
6 .... we found a good place to hide.

4 Order the words to make sentences in your notebook.

1 morning / raft / men / One / two / onto / ran / our
One morning, two men ran onto our raft.

2 wanted / from / escape / They / men / some / to
3 story / Nobody / the / knows / true
4 speak / him / preacher / to / The / asked
5 King / Everyone / stay / to / their / houses / wanted / the / in
6 money / King / the / the / counted / raft / On / his

5 **Write the correct answers in your notebook.**

Example: 1—b

1 Near the next town, they met . . .

  a a friendly dog.

  b a young man.

  c an English family.

2 Harvey's brother William . . .

  a is very ill.

  b died in England.

  c cannot hear anything.

3 "Our poor brother!" said the King, and he . . .

  a ran away.

  b started to cry.

  c shouted angrily.

4 "We're very happy to meet you," said Mary Jane. "Our uncle told us . . .

  a nothing about you."

  b a little about you."

  c all about you."

CHAPTER SIX

6 **Complete the sentences in your notebook with *and* or *but*.**

1 A woman came out of the kitchen, *and* she shouted at the dogs.

2 I told them all about the Sawyer family, ... I had a problem.

3 "It's a bad thing to help him, I know, ... I'm going to do it."

4 Tom came into the house, ... he kissed Aunt Sally!

5 Aunt Sally was very angry, ... she wanted to hit Tom.

6 Aunt Sally wanted to be angry about "Sid's" game, ... she was too happy.

7 **Complete these sentences in your notebook, using the prepositions from the box.**

> from   under   behind   to   towards   down

1 Jim's in a hut *behind* the house.
2 We'll take the key .... Uncle Silas's pants.
3 We'll go away .... the river.
4 Tom wrote the letter, and pushed it .... the door.
5 That night, fifteen men with guns came .... the house.
6 The dogs ran .... us.

CHAPTERS FOUR TO SEVEN

8 **Complete these sentences in your notebook, using the comparative or superlative forms from the box.**

> bigger   oldest   nearest   best   prettiest   easier

1 His *oldest* son came to America.
2 We were together on a small raft now, and it is .... to live with happy men.
3 The .... girls kissed him.
4 We stopped at a new place. I went into the .... town.
5 "You look much .... , and you're very different from your mother."
6 "I'll make a plan, too, and then we can choose the .... one."

Project work

1 You are one of these people. Write a diary page.
 • Jim in Chapter Three.
 • Mary Jane in Chapter Five.
 • Aunt Sally in Chapter Six.

2 Huck travels hundreds of miles down the Mississippi River. Make a map of the river and find out more about it. Make a presentation for your class.

3 Write about the people in the story. Who was good, bad, kind, etc.? Give reasons for your ideas.

4 Huck reads a book about George Washington. Who was he? Find out some things about his life and talk to the class about him.

5 The United States of America stopped having slaves in 1865. Find out more about this and write a report.

6 You are Peter Wilks. Write a letter to your two brothers in England.

7 Huck's dad was shot by someone in the house in the river. What happened, do you think? Write your own story about it.

An answer key for all questions and exercises can be found at **www.penguinreaders.co.uk**

Glossary

adventure (n.)
when you do something different
and it is exciting

aunt (n.)
the sister of your mother or father

blood (n.)
Blood is red. It is in your body.

dead (adj.)
not living

dig (v.)
to go into the ground

duke (n.)
A *duke* is a rich man. He is part
of a *king*'s family.

escape (v.)
to run away from
something bad

finally (adv.)
after a long time

free (adj.)
A *free* person is not a *slave*.

hide (v.)
You *hide* something because you
do not want people to find it.

king (n.)
A very important man in some
countries. He is very rich. His
family is rich and important, too.

mile (n.)
You can run a *mile* in about 7
to 10 minutes. A *mile* is about
1.61 kilometres long.

niece (n.)
the daughter of your brother
or sister

pirate (n.)
A *pirate* is a bad person. Pirates
work at sea. They stop other boats
and take things from them.

preacher (n.)
Preachers work in a church. They
tell stories about Jesus and *say*
prayers (= speak to God).

shoot (v.)
You *shoot* with a gun because you
want to hurt or kill someone.

slave (n.)
A *slave* works very hard for no
money. A *slave* cannot *escape*.

trick (v.)
Someone *tricks* you. Their words
are not true.

uncle (n.)
the brother of your mother
or father

way (n.)
how you do something

Penguin 🐧 Readers

Visit **www.penguinreaders.co.uk**
for FREE Penguin Readers resources
and digital and audio versions of this book.